D0328719

THE
PENIS
MIGHTIER
THAN THE
PENIS

for
CÉLINE HUGHES

THE
PENIS
MIGHTIER
THAN THE
PENIS

quadrille

〰〰〰〰〰〰〰〰〰〰〰

I HATE TO HEAR YOU TALK ABOUT ALL WOMEN AS IF THEY WERE FINE LADIES INSTEAD OF RATIONAL CREATURES. NONE OF US WANT TO BE IN CALM WATERS ALL OUR LIVES.

Persuasion (1817)

JANE AUSTEN

1775–1817

I THINK
HOUSEWORK
IS FAR MORE
TIRING AND
FRIGHTENING
THAN HUNTING,
NO COMPARISON,
AND YET AFTER
HUNTING WE HAD
EGGS FOR TEA AND
WERE MADE
TO REST FOR
HOURS,

BUT AFTER
HOUSEWORK
PEOPLE EXPECT
ONE TO GO ON
JUST AS IF
NOTHING SPECIAL
HAD HAPPENED.

The Pursuit of Love (1945)
NANCY MITFORD
1904–1973

WHISKY, GAMBLING AND FERRARIS ARE BETTER THAN HOUSEWORK.

FRANCOISE SAGAN
1934–2004

No black woman writer in this culture can write 'too much'. Indeed, no woman writer can write 'too much' ... No woman has ever written enough.

Remembered Rapture (1999)
BELL HOOKS
B.1952

In the new code of laws which I suppose it will be necessary for you to make, I desire you would remember the ladies, and be more generous and favourable to them than your ancestors ... Remember all men would be tyrants if they could.

Letter to John Adams (31 MARCH 1776)

ABIGAIL ADAMS

1744–1818

YES, INJURED WOMAN! RISE, ASSERT THY RIGHT!

The Rights of Woman
(WRITTEN 1795, PUBLISHED 1825)
ANNA LAETITIA BARBAULD
1743–1825

WOMEN ARE
SUPPOSED TO
BE VERY CALM
GENERALLY: BUT
WOMEN FEEL
JUST AS MEN
FEEL; THEY NEED
EXERCISE FOR
THEIR FACULTIES,
AND A FIELD FOR
THEIR EFFORTS AS
MUCH AS THEIR
BROTHERS DO;

THEY SUFFER
FROM TOO RIGID
A RESTRAINT,
TOO ABSOLUTE
A STAGNATION,
PRECISELY AS
MEN WOULD
SUFFER.

Jane Eyre (1847)
CHARLOTTE BRONTE
1816–55

IF ALL MEN ARE BORN FREE, HOW IS IT THAT ALL WOMEN ARE BORN SLAVES?

Some Reflections on Marriage (1706)

MARY ASTELL

1668–1731

I wrote because I could not help it. There was something that I wanted to say, and I said it: that was all.

Autobiography (1877)
HARRIET MARTINEAU
1802–76

SINCE WHEN WAS GENIUS FOUND RESPECTABLE?

Aurora Leigh (1857)

ELIZABETH BARRETT BROWNING

1806–61

A LITTLE ALARM NOW AND THEN KEEPS LIFE FROM STAGNATION.

Camilla (1796)

FANNY BURNEY

1752–1840

But for the most part, women are not educated as they should be, I mean those of quality; oft their education is only to dance, sing and fiddle, to write complemental letters, to read romances, to speak some languages that are not their native...

... their parents take more care of their feet than their head, more of their words than their reason.

Sociable Letters (1664)

MARGARET CAVENDISH

C.1624–74

THE HAPPIEST WOMEN, LIKE THE HAPPIEST NATIONS, HAVE NO HISTORY.

Mill on the Floss (1860)

GEORGE ELIOT

1819–80

THE GREATEST HEROES THAT THE WORLD CAN KNOW, TO *WOMEN* THEIR ORIGINAL MUST OWE.

THREE WISE SENTENCES *from the First Book of Esdras* (1740)

MARY COLLIER

C. 1690–C.1762

WHAT A
MISFORTUNE IT
IS TO BE BORN
A WOMAN!
WHY SEEK FOR
KNOWLEDGE,
WHICH CAN
PROVE ONLY
THAT OUR
WRETCHEDNESS
IS
IRREMEDIABLE?

IF A RAY OF LIGHT
BREAK UPON
US, IT IS BUT TO
MAKE DARKNESS
MORE VISIBLE;
TO SHOW US THE
NEW LIMITS,
THE GOTHIC
STRUCTURE, THE
IMPENETRABLE
BARRIERS OF
OUR PRISON.

Leonora (1806)

MARIA EDGEWORTH

1768–1849

WOMEN NEED NOT ALWAYS KEEP THEIR MOUTHS SHUT AND THEIR WOMBS OPEN.

Speech on the right to use contraceptives (1915)

EMMA GOLDMAN

1869–1940

You can wipe your feet on me, twist my motives around all you like, you can dump millstones in my head and drown me in the river, but you can't get me out of the story. I'm the plot, babe, and don't ever forget it.

Good Bones and Simple Murders (1982)

MARGARET ATWOOD

B.1939

BUT THE FRUIT
THAT CAN FALL
WITHOUT
SHAKING,
INDEED IS TOO
MELLOW
FOR ME.

A Collection of Poems (1758)
LADY MARY WORTLEY MONTAGU
1689–1762

WE ARE HERE TO CLAIM OUR RIGHT AS WOMEN, NOT ONLY TO BE FREE, BUT TO FIGHT FOR FREEDOM. THAT IT IS OUR RIGHT AS WELL AS OUR DUTY.

Votes for Women (SPEECH ON 31 MARCH 1911)
CHRISTABEL PANKHURST
1880–1958

I HAVE OFTEN
WISHED I HAD
TIME TO CULTIVATE
MODESTY... BUT I AM
TOO BUSY THINKING
ABOUT MYSELF.

INTERVIEW IN THE *Observer*
(30 APRIL 1950)

EDITH SITWELL
1887–1964

I WOULD HAVE
GIRLS REGARD
THEMSELVES NOT
AS ADJECTIVES,
BUT AS NOUNS.

Our Girls
(SPEECH, 1880)
ELIZABETH CADY STANTON
1815–1902

An impersonal and scientific
knowledge of the structure
of our bodies is the surest
safeguard against prurient
curiosity and
lascivious gloating.

Married Love (1912)
MARIE STOPES
1880–1958

YOU WERE ONCE WILD... DON'T LET THEM TAME YOU.

ISADORA DUNCAN
1877–1927

HERE LIES A
POOR WOMAN
WHO ALWAYS WAS
TIRED, FOR SHE
LIVED IN A PLACE
WHERE HELP WASN'T
HIRED. HER LAST
WORDS ON EARTH
WHERE, DEAR
FRIENDS, I AM GOING
WHERE WASHING AIN'T
DONE NOR SWEEPING
NOR SEWING,
AND EVERYTHING

THERE IS EXACT
TO MY WISHES,
FOR THERE THEY
DON'T EAT AND
THERE'S NO WASHING
OF DISHES...
DON'T MOURN FOR ME
NOW, DON'T MOURN
FOR ME NEVER,
FOR I'M GOING TO DO
NOTHING, FOR EVER
AND EVER.

Epitaph in Bushey churchyard
(BEFORE 1860; DESTROYED BY 1919)

I BELIEVE THAT
THE INFLUENCE
OF WOMEN
WILL SAVE
THE COUNTRY
BEFORE EVERY
OTHER POWER.

Speech in 1869
LUCY STONE
1818–93

I am a woman who enjoys herself very much; sometimes I lose, sometimes I win.

MATA HARI
1876–1917

From birth to 18 a girl needs good parents. From 18 to 35, she needs good looks. From 35 to 55, good personality. From 55 on, she needs good cash.

SOPHIE TUCKER
1887–1966

I LONG FOR
THE DAY MY SISTERS
WILL RISE, AND
OCCUPY THE SPHERE
TO WHICH THEY ARE
CALLED BY THEIR HIGH
NATURE AND DESTINY.

Speech in 1840
LUCRETIA MOTT
1793–1880

I DO NOT WISH THEM [WOMEN] TO HAVE POWER OVER MEN; BUT OVER THEMSELVES.

A Vindincation of the Rights of Women (1792)

MARY WOLLSTONECRAFT

1759–97

A MOTHER IS ALWAYS A MOTHER, SINCE A MOTHER IS A BIOLOGICAL FACT, WHILST A FATHER IS A MOVABLE FEAST.

Wise Children (1991)

ANGELA CARTER

1940–92

OLD FASHIONED WAYS WHICH NO LONGER APPLY TO CHANGED CONDITIONS ARE A SNARE IN WHICH THE FEET OF WOMEN HAVE ALWAYS BECOME READILY ENTANGLED.

Newer Ideas of Peace (1906)

JANE ADDAMS
1860–1935

THERE IS
A GREAT
DEAL OF
UNMAPPED
COUNTRY
WITHIN US.

Daniel Deronda
GEORGE ELIOT
1819–80

I BEND MY KNEE TO NO MAN UNLESS I CHOOSE TO.

CATARINA SFROZA
1463–1509

Don't shut yourself up in a band box because you are a woman, but understand what is going on, and educate yourself to take part in the world's work, for it all affects you and yours.

Little Women (1869)
Louisa May Alcott
US NOVELIST
1832–88

I WOULD THEREFORE
EXHORT ALL MY SEX...
TO BETAKE THEMSELVES
TO THE IMPROVEMENT
OF THEIR MINDS
AND SHOW OURSELVES
WORTHY.

*Woman not inferior to Man: or a Short and
Modest Vindication of the Natural Right of
the Fair Sex to a Perfect Equality of Power,
Dignity and Esteem with the Men* (1739)

LADY SOPHIA FERMOR

1721–45

I WILL BE CALM. I WILL BE MISTRESS OF MYSELF.

Sense and Sensibility (1811)

JANE AUSTEN

1775–1817

WIT"S EMPIRE NOW SHALL KNOW A FEMALE REIGN.

The Emulation (1703)
SARAH EGERTON
1670–1723

A WOMAN WITH A MIND IS FIT FOR ANY TASK.

The City of Women (1404)
CHRISTINE DE PIZAN
1364–1430

〜〜〜〜〜〜〜〜〜〜〜〜〜

I AM NOT AFRAID OF STORMS FOR I AM LEARNING HOW TO SAIL MY SHIP.

Little Women (1857)

LOUISA MAY ALCOTT

1832–88

MY DREAMS WERE ALL MY OWN; I ACCOUNTED FOR THEM TO NOBODY; THEY WERE MY REFUGE WHEN ANNOYED — MY DEAREST PLEASURE WHEN FREE.

PREFACE TO *Frankenstein* (1831)
MARY SHELLEY
1797–1851

A MAN IS SO IN THE WAY IN THE HOUSE.

Cranford (1853)

ELIZABETH GASKELL

1810–65

The more I study,
the more insatiable
do I feel my genius
for it to be.

ADA LOVELACE
1815–52

OUGHT NOT EVERY WOMAN, LIKE EVERY MAN, FOLLOW THE BENT OF HER TALENTS?

Corinne (1807)

ANNE LOUISE GERMAINE DE STAËL

1766–1817

I AM ONLY ONE,
BUT STILL I AM ONE.
I CANNOT DO
EVERYTHING,
BUT STILL I CAN
DO SOMETHING.
I WILL NOT REFUSE
TO DO THE
SOMETHING
I CAN DO.

HELEN KELLER
1880–1968

I SLEPT AND
DREAMED THAT
LIFE WAS BEAUTY;
I WOKE AND
FOUND THAT LIFE
WAS DUTY.

Beauty and Duty (1840)
ELLEN STURGIS HOOPER
1816–41

I MARRIED BENEATH ME. ALL WOMEN DO.

VISCOUNTESS ASTOR
1879–1964

Then that little man in black there, he says women can't have as much rights as men, 'cause Christ wasn't a woman! Where did your Christ come from?

FROM GOD AND A WOMAN! MAN HAD NOTHING TO DO WITH HIM.

Speech during the Ohio Women's Rights Convention, 1851

SOJOURNER TRUTH

C.1797–1883

NO MATTER WHAT YOUR FIGHT, DON'T BE LADYLIKE.

MOTHER JONES
1837–1930

*Women must try to do things
as men have tried.
When they fail, their failure
must be but a challenge
to others.*

AMELIA EARHEART

1897–1937

BUT WHATEVER CAME, SHE HAD RESOLVED NEVER AGAIN TO BELONG TO ANOTHER THAN HERSELF.

The Awakening (1899)
KATE CHOPIN
1850–1904

LIFE IS ALWAYS A TIGHTROPE OR A FEATHER BED. GIVE ME THE TIGHTROPE.

Journal entry, MARCH 1926
EDITH WHARTON
1862–1937

PATIENCE IS MORE WORTHY THAN MIRACLE-WORKING.

MARGERY KEMPE
1373–1438

WE CANNOT STAY HOME ALL OUR LIVES, WE MUST PRESENT OURSELVES TO THE WORLD AND WE MUST LOOK UPON IT AS AN ADVENTURE.

BEATRIX POTTER
1866–1943

*How many women
might the history be
comprised in those
few words —
she lived, suffered
and was buried!*

*Characteristics of Women, moral,
political and historical* (1832)
ANNA BROWNELL
JAMESON
1794–1860

I HONOUR EVERY
WOMAN WHO HAS
STRENGTH ENOUGH
TO STEP OUT OF THE
BEATEN PATH WHEN
SHE FEELS THAT
HER WALK LIES IN
ANOTHER.

HARRIET HOSMER
1830–1908

I AM A PRINCESS. ALL GIRLS ARE. EVEN IF THEY LIVE IN TINY OLD ATTICS. EVEN IF THEY DRESS IN RAGS, EVEN IF THEY AREN'T PRETTY OR SMART OR YOUNG. THEY'RE STILL PRINCESSES.

A Little Princess (1905)
FRANCES HODGSON BURNETT
1849–1924

TO BE RUDE IS AS GOOD AS BEING CLEVER.

LAETITIA ELIZABETH LANDON
1802–38

BE GLAD.
BE GOOD.
BE BRAVE.

Pollyanna (1913)

ELEANOR PORTER

1867–1920

SOME PEOPLE GO THROUGH LIFE TRYING TO FIND OUT WHAT THE WORLD HOLDS FOR THEM, ONLY TO FIND OUT TOO LATE THAT IT'S WHAT THEY BRING TO THE WORLD THAT COUNTS.

Anne of Green Gables (1908)
LUCY MAUD MONTGOMERY
1874–1942

IF MEN COULD
SEE US AS WE
REALLY ARE,
THEY WOULD
BE A LITTLE
AMAZED; BUT THE
CLEVEREST,
THE ACUTEST
MEN ARE OFTEN
UNDER AN
ILLUSION ABOUT
WOMEN: THEY
DO NOT READ
THEM IN A TRUE

LIGHT: THEY
MISAPPREHEND
THEM, BOTH FOR
GOOD AND EVIL:
THEIR GOOD
WOMAN IS A
QUEER THING,
HALF DOLL, HALF
ANGEL; THEIR
BAD WOMAN
ALMOST ALWAYS
A FIEND.

Shirley (1849)
CHARLOTTE BRONTE
1816–55

FEMINISM HASN'T FAILED, IT'S JUST NEVER BEEN TRIED.

An Experiment in Love (1995)

HILARY MANTEL

B.1952

THIS IS A BATTLE THAT WE WILL WIN. BECAUSE WOMEN ARE WITTIER, BRIGHTER, STRONGER AND BRAVER THAN A MISOGYNISTIC AND PARTRIARCHAL WORLD HAS GIVEN US CREDIT FOR.

Everyday Sexism (2014)
LAURA BATES
B.1986

WOMEN AND ELEPHANTS NEVER FORGET.

'BALLADE OF UNFORTUNATE MAMMALS'

The Complete Poems of Dorothy Parker (1994)

DOROTHY PARKER

1893–1967

YOU ARE EXTRAORDINARY WITHIN YOUR LIMITS, BUT YOUR LIMITS ARE EXTRAORDINARY!

Everybody's Autobiography (1937)

GERTRUDE STEIN

1874–1946

I THINK THE GIRL
WHO IS ABLE TO
EARN HER OWN LIVING
AND PAY HER OWN WAY
SHOULD BE AS HAPPY AS
ANYBODY ON EARTH.
THE SENSE OF
INDEPENDENCE
AND SECURITY IS
VERY SWEET.

INTERVIEW IN THE *New York Press* (1905)
SUSAN B. ANTHONY
1820–1906

AS LONG AS SHE THINKS OF A MAN, NOBODY OBJECTS TO A WOMAN THINKING.

Orlando (1928)

VIRGINIA WOOLF

1882–1942

WHAT IS SAD FOR
WOMEN OF MY
GENERATION
IS THAT THEY
WEREN'T
SUPPOSED TO
WORK IF THEY
HAD FAMILIES.

WHAT WERE
THEY GOING TO
DO WHEN THE
CHILDREN ARE
GROWN – WATCH
THE RAINDROPS
COMING DOWN
THE WINDOW
PANE?

(1962)

**JAQUELINE KENNEDY
ONASSIS**
1929–1994

MEN FIGHT WARS. WOMEN WIN THEM.

ELIZABETH I
1553–1603

*A woman of honour
should never suspect another
of things she
would not do herself.*

Memoirs (1628)
MARGARET DE VALOIS
1553–1615

FEET, WHAT DO I NEED YOU FOR WHEN I HAVE WINGS TO FLY?

FRIDA KAHLO
1907–54

THERE IS NOT A FEMALE MIND. THE BRAIN IS NOT AN ORGAN OF SEX. ONE MIGHT AS WELL SPEAK OF A FEMALE LIVER.

Women and Economics (1898)
CHARLOTTE PERKINS GILLMAN
1860–1935

ABOVE ALL, BE THE HEROINE OF YOUR OWN LIFE, NOT THE VICTIM.

Wellesley Address (1996)

NORA EPHRON

1941–2012

THERE IS NOTHING SO ABSOLUTELY BRACING FOR THE SOUL AS THE FREQUENT TURNING OF ONE'S BACK ON DUTIES.

The Adventures of Elizabeth in Rügen (1904)

ELIZABETH VON ARNIM

1866–1941

How wonderful it is that
nobody need wait a single
moment before starting to
improve the world.

The Diary of a Young Girl (1947)
ANNE FRANK
1929–45

THEY ARE INCONVENIENTLY REASONABLE, THESE WOMEN

Herland (1915)

CHARLOTTE PERKINS GILMAN

1860–1935

It really is something … that men disapprove even of our doing things that are patently good. Wouldn't it be possible for us just to banish these men from our lives, and escape their carping and jeering once and for all? Couldn't we live without them?

COULDN'T WE EARN OUR LIVING AND MANAGE OUR AFFAIRS WITHOUT HELP FROM THEM? COME ON, LET'S WAKE UP, AND CLAIM BACK OUR FREEDOM, AND THE HONOUR AND DIGNITY THAT THEY HAVE USURPED FROM US FOR SO LONG.

The Worth of Women (1600)
MODERATA FONTE
1555–92

WHATEVER WOMEN DO, THEY MUST DO TWICE AS WELL AS MEN TO BE THOUGHT HALF AS GOOD. LUCKILY, THIS IS NOT DIFFICULT.

Speech on becoming Mayor of Ottowa (1951)

CHARLOTTE WHITTON

(1896–1975)

OH, LET US LOSE OUR MILK TEETH AND CUT INSTEAD THE STRONG TEETH OF HATE AND LOVE.

St Catherine of Siena
1347–80

◇◇◇

WE ARE
NOT REALLY
SENSELESS,
AND WE ARE NOT
ANGELS, TOO,
BUT VERY HUMAN
BEINGS, HUMAN
JUST AS MUCH
AS YOU.
IT'S HARD UPON
OCCASIONS TO

◇◇◇

BE FORCEFUL AND SUBLIME WHEN YOU'RE TREATED AS INCOMPETENTS THREE-QUARTERS OF THE TIME.

Are Women People? (1915)
ALICE DUER MILLER
(1874–1942)

I GET ANGRY ABOUT THINGS, THEN GO ON AND WORK.

INTERVIEW WITH *Salon*

TONI MORRISON

B.1931

ROLL UP YOUR SLEEVES, SET YOUR MIND TO MAKING HISTORY AND WAGE SUCH A FIGHT FOR LIBERTY THAT THE WHOLE WORLD WILL RESPECT YOUR SEX.

CARRIE CHAPMAN CATT
1859–1947

I WILL
WORK IN
MY
OWN WAY,
ACCORDING
TO THE
LIGHT THAT
IS IN ME.

LYDIA M. CHILD
1802–80

THE FACT THAT I WAS A GIRL NEVER DAMAGED MY AMBITIONS TO BE A POPE OR AN EMPEROR.

The World and the Parish (1970)

WILLA CATHER

1873–1947

YOU'RE
ONLY A MAN!
YOU'VE NOT
OUR GIFTS!
I CAN TELL
YOU! WHY, A
WOMAN CAN
THINK OF

A HUNDRED DIFFERENT THINGS AT ONCE, ALL OF THEM CONTRADICTORY!

Powder and Patch (1923)

GEORGETTE HEYER

1902–74

WHEN GOD MADE MAN, SHE WAS PRACTICING.

Cat on the Scent (1999),
RITA MAE BROWN
B. 1944

WHY DO GENTLEMEN'S VOICES CARRY SO CLEARLY, WHEN WOMEN'S ARE SO EASILY STIFLED?

Affinity (1999)
SARAH WATERS
B.1966

I EMBRACE THE
LABEL OF BAD
FEMINIST BECAUSE
I AM HUMAN.
I AM MESSY.
I AM NOT TRYING
TO BE AN EXAMPLE.
I AM NOT TRYING
TO BE PERFECT.
I AM NOT TRYING
TO SAY I HAVE ALL
THE ANSWERS.

I AM NOT TRYING
TO SAY I'M RIGHT.
I'M JUST TRYING,
TRYING TO
SUPPORT WHAT I
BELIEVE IN, TRYING
TO DO SOME GOOD
IN THIS WORLD.

Bad Feminist (2014)

ROXANE GAY

B.1974

I'M A
FEMINIST.
I'VE BEEN
A FEMALE FOR
A LONG
TIME NOW.
IT'D BE STUPID
NOT TO
BE ON MY
OWN SIDE.

MAYA ANGELOU
1928–2014

NOLITE BASTARDES CARBODORUM

DON"T LET THE BASTARDS GRIND YOU DOWN

The Handmaid's Tale (1985),
MARGARET ATWOOD
B.1939

I MYSELF HAVE NEVER
BEEN ABLE TO FIND
OUT PRECISELY WHAT
FEMINISM IS: I ONLY
KNOW THAT PEOPLE
CALL ME A FEMINIST
WHENEVER I EXPRESS
SENTIMENTS THAT
DIFFERENTIATE ME
FROM A DOORMAT.

The Young Rebecca, Writings 1911-1917
(1982)
REBECCA WEST
1892–1983

DON'T LET THEM GET YOU DOWN. BE CHEEKY. AND WILD. AND WONDERFUL.

Pippi Longstocking (1945)
ASTRID LINDGREN
1907–2002

WHAT WOULD HAPPEN IF ONE WOMAN TOLD THE TRUTH ABOUT HER LIFE? THE WORLD WOULD SPLIT OPEN.

MURIEL RUKEYSER
1913–80

May I write
words more
naked
than flesh
stronger than
bone, more
resilient
than sinew,
sensitive
than nerve.

Sappho
0611–0569

THERE IS NO GREATER AGONY THAN BEARING AN UNTOLD STORY INSIDE YOU.

Dust Tracks on the Road (1942)
ZORA NEALE HURSTON
1891–1960

I am furious about
Women's Liberationists.
They keep getting up on soap
boxes and proclaiming that
women are brighter than
men. That's true, but it
should be kept very
quiet or it ruins the
whole racket.

ANITA LOOS
1889–1981

AH, MEN
WHY DO YOU WANT
ALL THIS ATTENTION?
I CAN WRITE POEMS FOR
MYSELF, MAKE
LOVE TO A DOORKNOB IF
ABSOLUTELY
NECESSARY, WHAT DO
YOU HAVE TO OFFER ME I
CAN'T FIND OTHERWISE
EXCEPT HUMILIATION?
WHICH I NO
LONGER NEED.

'AGING FEMALE POET SITS ON THE BALCONY'
Poems II 1976–1986
MARGARET ATWOOD
B.1939

I AM NOT A
TENTATIVE
PERSON.
WHATEVER
I DO,
I GIVE UP MY
WHOLE SELF
FOR IT.

Letters

EDNA ST VINCENT MILLAY

1892–1950

I USED TO THINK,
WHAT DO YOU
THINK FEMINISM IS,
LADIES? WHAT PART
OF "LIBERATION FOR
WOMEN" IS NOT FOR
YOU? IS IT FREEDOM
TO VOTE? THE RIGHT
NOT TO BE OWNED BY
THE MAN YOU MARRY?
THE CAMPAIGN FOR
EQUAL PAY? "VOGUE"

BY MADONNA? JEANS?
DID ALL THAT GOOD
SHIT **GET ON YOUR
NERVES?** OR WERE
YOU JUST **DRUNK AT
THE TIME OF THE
SURVEY?**

How to be a Woman (2011)
CAITLIN MORAN
B. 1975

I am patient with stupidity,
but not with those who are
proud of it.

The Last Years of a Rebel (1967)
EDITH SITWELL
1887–1964

REMEMBER, IF PEOPLE TALK BEHIND YOUR BACK IT IS ONLY BECAUSE YOU ARE TWO STEPS AHEAD OF THEM.

Fried Green Tomatoes at the Whistle Stop Café (1987)

FANNIE FLAGG

B.1944

HIS NAME WAS
PRIVILEGE,
BUT HERS WAS
POSSIBILITY.
HIS WAS THE
SAME OLD STORY,
BUT HERS WAS A
NEW ONE ABOUT
THE POSSIBILITY
OF CHANGING
A STORY THAT
REMAINS
UNFINISHED,

THAT INCLUDES
ALL OF US, THAT
MATTERS SO
MUCH, THAT
WE WILL WATCH
BUT ALSO MAKE
AND TELL IN THE
WEEKS, MONTHS,
YEARS, DECADES
TO COME.

Men Explain Things to Me (2014)
REBECCA SOLNIT
B.1961

LIFE IS TOO SHORT TO STUFF A MUSHROOM.

Superwoman (1975)
SHIRLEY CONRAN
B.1952

I THINK BEING A
WOMAN IS LIKE
BEING IRISH...
EVERYONE
SAYS YOU'RE
IMPORTANT AND
NICE, BUT YOU
TAKE SECOND
PLACE ALL THE
TIME.

A Severed Head (1971)
IRIS MURDOCH
1919–99

IT IS BECAUSE I'M A FEMINIST THAT I CAN'T STAND WOMEN LIMITING OTHER WOMEN'S IMAGINATIONS. IT REALLY MAKES ME ANGRY.

INTERVIEW WITH *Salon* (1996)

A.S. BYATT

B.1936

A WOMAN, WHEN SHE IS HEROIC, IS NOT HEROIC BY HALVES

GEORGE SAND
1804–76

REFORM IS BORN OF NEED, NOT OF PITY.

Life in the Iron Mills (1861)
REBECCA HARDING DAVIS
1831–1910

SUCCESS IS NEVER SO INTERESTING AS STRUGGLE.

Death comes to the Archbishop (1927)

WILLA CATHER

1873–1947

NEVER
WOUND
A SNAKE;
KILL IT.

HARRIET TUBMAN
DIED 1913

SO MUCH HAS BEEN SAID AND SUNG OF BEAUTIFUL YOUNG GIRLS, WHY DOESN'T SOMEONE WAKE UP TO THE BEAUTY OF OLD WOMEN?

HARRIET BEECHER STOWE
1811–96

I KNOW NOTHING OF
MAN'S RIGHTS, OR
WOMEN'S RIGHTS,
HUMAN RIGHTS ARE
ALL THAT I
RECOGNISE.

*Letters on the Equality of the Sexes
and the Condition of Women* (1838)

SARAH GRIMKE

1792–1873

I DON'T WANT TO MAKE SOMEBODY ELSE. I WANT TO MAKE MYSELF.

Sula (1973)

TONI MORRISON

B. 1931

JUST BREATHING ISN'T LIVING!

Pollyanna (1913)

ELEANOR PORTER

1867–1920

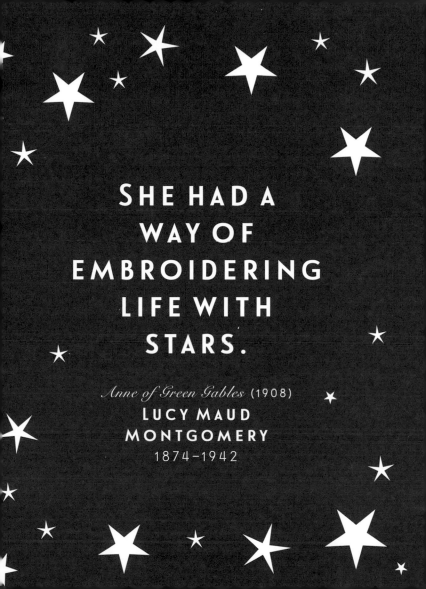

SHE HAD A WAY OF EMBROIDERING LIFE WITH STARS.

Anne of Green Gables (1908)

LUCY MAUD MONTGOMERY

1874–1942

I'M A WRITER FIRST AND A WOMAN AFTER.

Journal of Katherine Mansfield (1927)

KATHERINE MANSFIELD

1888–1923

KEEP AN EYE ON YOUR INNER WORLD AND KEEP AWAY FROM ADS, IDIOTS AND MOVIE STARS.

INTERVIEW IN *Slate* (2002)

DOROTHEA TANNING

1910–2012

THE EXTRAORDINARY
WOMAN DEPENDS ON
THE ORDINARY WOMAN.
IT IS ONLY WHEN WE
KNOW WHAT WERE THE
CONDITIONS OF THE
AVERAGE WOMAN'S
LIFE – THE NUMBER OF
CHILDREN, WHETHER
SHE HAD MONEY OF HER
OWN, IF SHE HAD A ROOM
TO HERSELF, WHETHER
SHE HAD HELP BRINGING
UP HER FAMILY, IF SHE
HAD SERVANTS,

WHETHER PART OF
OF THE HOUSEWORK
WAS HER TASK — IT IS
ONLY WHEN WE CAN
MEASURE THE WAY OF
LIFE AND EXPERIENCE
MADE POSSIBLE TO THE
ORDINARY WOMAN THAT
WE CAN ACCOUNT FOR
THE SUCCESS OR FAILURE
OF THE EXTRAORDINARY
WOMAN AS A WRITER.

A Room of One's Own (1929)
VIRGINIA WOOLF
1882–1941

YOUR FEMINIST PREMISE SHOULD BE: I MATTER. I MATTER EQUALLY. NOT 'IF ONLY'. NOT 'AS LONG AS'. I MATTER EQUALLY. FULL STOP.

Dear Ijeawele, or a Feminist Manifesto in Fifteen Suggestions (2017)

CHIMAMANDA NGOZI ADICHE

B.1977

LADIES, THERE IS NO NEUTRAL POSITION FOR US TO ASSUME.

The Mother Of Us All (OPERA) (1947)

GERTRUDE STEIN

1874–1946

*There are as many
sorts of women as there
are women.*

The Tale of Genji (C. 1021)
MURASAKI SHIKIBU
973–1014

SHE BURNED TOO BRIGHT FOR THIS WORLD.

Wuthering Heights (1847)

EMILY BRONTE

1818–48

Publishing Director Sarah Lavelle
Project Editor Susannah Otter
Designer Maeve Bargman
Production Director Vincent Smith
Production Controller Jessica Otway

Published in 2018 by Quadrille,
an imprint of Hardie Grant Publishing

Quadrille
52–54 Southwark Street
London SE1 1UN
quadrille.com

Cataloguing in Publication Data: a catalogue record for this book
is available from the British Library.

design © Quadrille 2017

ISBN 9781787131866

Printed and bound at Toppan Leefung, DongGuan City, China